God's Peaceful Reminders

A DEVOTIONAL

Amy Hille

WESTBOW
PRESS®
A DIVISION OF THOMAS NELSON
& ZONDERVAN

WestBow Press books may be ordered through booksellers or by contacting:

WestBow Press
A Division of Thomas Nelson & Zondervan
1663 Liberty Drive
Bloomington, IN 47403
www.westbowpress.com
844-714-3454

ISBN: 979-8-3850-0415-7 (sc)
ISBN: 979-8-3850-0416-4 (hc)
ISBN: 979-8-3850-0417-1 (e)

Library of Congress Control Number: 2023914400

Print information available on the last page.

WestBow Press rev. date: 10/24/2023

DAY 1
Number Your Days

Our lives last seventy years or, if we are strong, eighty years. Even the best of them are struggle and sorrow; indeed, they pass quickly and we fly away.
—Psalm 90:10 (NLT)

Have you ever thought about years in days? If you live to be seventy years old, that is equivalent to 25,550 days. This number makes me realize how fast life goes by. I want to make sure that I spend each day well. Each day should be spent with others, helping, encouraging, and most of all, loving one another well. When I break the years into days, I realize how short and precious life really is.

I was only supposed to live twenty minutes. I was born three months premature. I weighed only two pounds. I am now forty-three years old. Thank you, God, for each day you have given me. Please give me more days on this earth so that I can continue to complete your work and enjoy time with my family and friends. Psalm 118:24 says it best: "This is the day that the Lord has made; let us rejoice and be glad in it." How can you use these days well to serve God?

DAY 2
Your Life's Purpose

*Seek the Kingdom of God above all else, and live
righteously, and he will give you everything you need.*
—MATTHEW 6:33 (NLT)

God will give you everything you need. Figure out your purpose
in life and do it, regardless of what others say. Do it for God. Do
it for you. God has given you precious minutes to live. God wants you
to enjoy life by spending time with others, laughing, singing, traveling
the world, enjoying food, and playing with children. Spend time with
friends, go on dates with your spouse, and sit face-to-face with others
instead of texting them on your phone.

God wanted me to write this devotional. I have wanted to write it
for over ten years. God gave me everything I needed. I just need to trust
him. Matthew 7:7 says, "Keep on asking and you will receive what you
ask for. Keep on seeking, and you will find. Keep on knocking, and the
door will be opened to you." Pray to God often. Ask him what he wants
you to do with your life. Then listen to his answer. What is God telling
you to do on this earth? Ponder that for a minute.

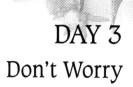

DAY 3
Don't Worry

Give all your worries and cares to God, for he cares about you.
—1 Peter 5:7 (NLT)

Someone once told me that worrying is praying for what you don't want. That stopped me in my tracks. Instead, pray for what you want in your life. Focus on what you want instead of what you don't want. Even Jesus said not to worry about life. Trust Jesus. Each of us has worries in this life. We need to learn to give all our worries to God. God wants us to enjoy life instead of being filled with worry. When you find yourself worrying about tomorrow, stop and give it to God. God cares for you deeply, so talk to him often. He wants a relationship with you every day.

Matthew 6:34 says, "So don't worry about tomorrow, for tomorrow will bring its own worries. Today's trouble is enough for today." God is telling us to live in the moment. Be present today. Focus on today. In today's world, everyone is so focused on what's next. Instead, focus on today. Enjoy today. What is one thing you are worrying about today? I encourage you to let go of that worry to God.

DAY 4
Don't Give Up

Be on guard. Stand firm in the faith. Be courageous.
Be strong. And do everything with love.
—1 Corinthians 16:13–14 (NLT)

For the past nine years, I have been obsessed with learning everything I can about the Bible. I am also obsessed with teaching my children about the Bible. I was so excited when I bought the kids their own Bibles for Christmas. Unfortunately, they were not as excited as I was. In the Catholic Bible, there are seventy-three books. I read all of them in nineteen months. There were many times when I wanted to give up. I wanted to give up because reading the Bible was challenging. During the difficult times of reading, I sometimes felt like Satan was in my ear telling me to give up because it was hard. I told Satan to go away. Of course, he wants me to stop learning about Jesus and God's plan. Let me restate the verse, "Be on guard. Stand firm in the faith. Be courageous. Be strong." Remember that the light always defeats the darkness. Was there a time when you wanted to give up because life got too hard? How did you overcome it?

DAY 5
Temper Tantrums

*Understand this, my dear brothers and sisters: You must all be
quick to listen, slow to speak, and slow to get angry. Human
anger does not produce the righteousness God desires.*

—JAMES 1:19–20 (NLT)

When I was a child, I had a terrible temper. My temper would get the best of me when playing card games with my family. If I was losing the game, my temper appeared. I hate to say this, but I am easily angered when playing card games as an adult too. I can't help myself, but God can help me with this weakness of mine. God says we should be slow to anger. Do you get angry easily? The next time you feel yourself getting angry, say to yourself, *Slow to anger.* If you want to be righteous before God, be slow to anger.

The Bible also tells us to be quick to listen and slow to speak. This is another weakness of mine. I feel like I interrupt others often because I want to be quick to answer the question. However, I should do the opposite—be quick to listen and slow to speak. James 1:22 says, "But don't just listen to God's word. You must do what it says." I love reading God's Word, but do I do what his Word says, or do I follow my own way? Sometimes we get trapped into doing things our own way because it's easier. God challenges us to listen to his Word and do what it says. What are some of your weaknesses? Ask God to help you overcome your weaknesses.

DAY 6
Joy and Peace

I pray that God, the source of hope, will fill you completely with joy and peace because you trust in him. Then you will overflow with confident hope through the power of the Holy Spirit.
—ROMANS 15:13 (NLT)

There were three days in my life when I felt the most joy and peace: my wedding day, the day my son was born, and the day my daughter was born. God filled me completely with joy and peace on those three days. These blessings make me trust God even more. He gave me the best gifts. I prayed for these gifts for many years. I am so grateful that God gave them to me.

Romans 15:2 says, "We should help others do what is right and build them up in the Lord." Being a parent of two beautiful children is a gift from God. God says that we should help others do what is right and build them up in the Lord. As a family, we go to church every Sunday. We pray for grace before dinner. I read devotionals to the kids before bed. As a parent, I need to teach my children about God. I need to teach them right from wrong. God wants us to be great teachers. How can you be a great teacher to someone today? Can you recall any days when God filled you with complete joy and peace? Reflect on those days now.

DAY 7
Challenging Seasons

*Don't worry about anything instead, pray about everything.
Tell God what you need, and thank him for all he has done.*
—Philippians 4:6 (NLT)

I have had many seasons of worry in my life. When I was born, I was only supposed to live for twenty minutes. When I was in kindergarten, I had a lazy eye. In college, I walked away from pharmacy school without a plan. In my mid-twenties, I had a bleeding tumor in my colon, and I was diagnosed with hepatitis C. I was also diagnosed with rheumatoid arthritis.

We all have challenging seasons. Instead of worrying through these challenging times, I pray. The verse says, "Tell God what you need, and thank him for all he has done." God will listen to your needs. Thank God for everything he has done for you. When I was first diagnosed with hepatitis C, I worried endlessly. I worried that I gave it to my husband. I worried that it was not treatable. I worried about how sick I would get. But then I listened to God and prayed, which helped ease my worry. Let God give you peace.

Have you had seasons of worry? How did you handle those seasons of life? How can you give thanks to God today? Philippians 4:13 says, "For I can do everything through Christ, who gives me strength." God gave me strength during these difficult seasons of life. God walked with me, and sometimes he carried me. He never left my side. What seasons of life has God helped you through?

DAY 8
Difficult Times

*Always be joyful. Never stop praying. Be thankful in all circumstances,
for this is God's will for you who belong to Christ Jesus.*
—1 THESSALONIANS 5:16–18 (NLT)

When I was in my twenties, I was diagnosed with rheumatoid arthritis. Over the years, I have had joint and back pain. The pain got so bad that I had to go on IV infusions. I was on infusions for nine years. My insurance changed one year, and I had to see a different rheumatologist. It turns out that I had been misdiagnosed, and all my symptoms were from my hepatitis C. I was in shock that I did not have rheumatoid arthritis. That day was full of mixed emotions. I cried so many tears because my rheumatologist said she would discontinue my IV infusions immediately. I was so scared that my joint pain would return even worse, but I was happy that I did not have rheumatoid arthritis. I was disappointed that I had been misdiagnosed for so many years.

God says, "Be thankful in all circumstances." Even though my circumstances were confusing at first, I needed to be thankful. God also says, "Always be joyful. Never stop praying." During this difficult and confusing time, I don't remember being joyful. I do remember praying a lot. Here is another example of reading and then doing God's Word. I need to practice doing God's Word in all situations, even the difficult ones. Have you ever gone through something difficult? How did God help you through this difficult time?

DAY 9
Sad Moments

God blesses those who mourn, for they will be comforted.
—MATTHEW 5:4 (NLT)

E veryone has sad moments in life. Just know that God will comfort you during these difficult times. In the summer of 1999, it was extremely hard to lose my grandma. I will never forget seeing the ambulance across the road from my parents' house in the middle of the night. My grandma had a stroke. I remember seeing her in the hospital and then the nursing home. She never made it home after that. I am still sad twenty-two years later, but God brings me comfort. I wish I could hug her again and tell her I love her. I know she is watching over me each day. God has provided me comfort over the years as I have mourned.

We can always count on God to help us through our sad moments in life. Psalm 34:18 says, "The Lord is close to the brokenhearted; he rescues those whose spirits are crushed." And Isaiah 41:10 says, "Don't be afraid, for I am with you. Don't be discouraged, for I am your God. I will strengthen you and help you. I will hold you up with my victorious right hand." These verses should give us a lot of comfort. God will help us through all our sad moments. He is there comforting and strengthening us. I don't know about you, but that gives me a lot of hope to get through the sad moments of the past and future. Do you have a sad moment in your life that still bothers you? Ask God to help you through it.

DAY 10
Spread Kindness

Kind words are like honey—sweet to the soul and healthy for the body.
—Proverbs 16:24 (NLT)

We always hear people say, "Be kind to each other." This statement comes from Ephesians 4:32, which says, "Instead, be kind to each other, tenderhearted, forgiving one another, just as God through Christ has forgiven you." We should try to do acts of kindness every day. This can make the world a happier place for everyone. The definition of kindness is "the quality of being friendly, generous, and considerate." (1) How kind are you to others throughout the day?

When my eight-year-old son and I would go grocery shopping, he would say, "Have a good day," to everyone we passed. That simple statement made so many people smile. He made their day with that simple gesture, and he also made my day. Smiles are contagious, and seeing so many smiles during our one-hour shopping trip was heartwarming. I will never forget that day. My son spread kindness around like confetti. How can you spread kindness around like confetti today?

DAY 11
Involve God

Take delight in the Lord, and he will give you your heart's desires.
Commit everything you do to the Lord. Trust him, and he will help you.
—Psalm 37:4–5 (NLT)

What dreams do you have for yourself or your family? Ask God, and he will help you achieve them. One of my dreams is to travel with my husband. I would love to see Paris and Hawaii. Next summer, our family wants to go to Nashville, Tennessee. Do you have any trips planned for your family? We should chase our hearts' desires. Go chase your dreams and make them happen with God's help.

Psalm 20:4 says, "May he grant your heart's desires and make all your plans succeed." God wants what is best for you. He wants to listen to your heart's desires and guide you so that all your plans succeed. Do you talk regularly with God about your heart's desires? Psalm 37 says, "Trust him, and he will help you." Talk to God about your heart's desires and not only your struggles in life. God wants to know your heart. God wants you to be happy.

The opening verse says, "Commit everything you do to the Lord." When we do our daily chores, work at our careers, and care for our families, we should do it all for God. Colossians 3:23 says, "Work willingly at whatever you do, as though you were working for the Lord rather than for people." We need to involve God into our working days. We need to thank him for helping us through each day. Even though our days may seem exhausting at times, we need to give thanks to God for another day on this earth. Each day is a gift from God, and we should not take it for granted. How can you involve God more into your day-to-day activities?

DAY 12
Reflect

And people should eat and drink and enjoy the fruits of their labor, for these are gifts from God.
—Ecclesiastes 3:13 (NLT)

God provides us with many gifts. Try to enjoy each day, even the challenging ones. On challenging days, we need to step back and try to enjoy the fruits of our labor.

I love the holidays. It's a time to eat, drink, and be merry. During the holidays, we love spending time with family and enjoying a delicious meal together. I love all our great conversations and playing bingo together. The holidays make me very happy.

What makes you happy? Ecclesiastes 9:7 says, "So go ahead. Eat your food with joy, and drink your wine with a happy heart, for God approves of this!" God says we should work hard in this life, but he also says that we should enjoy life. Take time to rest, go on vacation with your family, and reflect on this wonderful life. Psalm 128:2 says, "You will enjoy the fruit of your labor. How joyful and prosperous you will be!" It feels good to accomplish a task or a job. God wants us to feel good about all that we accomplished and all that we will accomplish. Be joyful. Be grateful for the gifts God gives us. Reflect on all the gifts God has already given you.

DAY 13
Learn and Grow

I prayed to the Lord, and he answered me.
He freed me from all my fears.
—Psalm 34:4 (NLT)

In 2020, I lived in a lot of fear due to the COVID-19 pandemic. Our family did not go out in public very much. We watched church online. We did not go into any stores for one year. We only did online ordering and pickup. It was hard not seeing any family or friends during this time. God watched over us, and we prayed a lot. We ended up with COVID-19 in 2021. We were lucky to have mild symptoms. Thank you, God, for taking care of us during this difficult time.

Did you feel isolated during the COVID-19 pandemic? Isaiah 43:2 says, "When you go through deep waters, I will be with you. When you go through rivers of difficulty, you will not drown. When you walk through the fire of oppression, you will not be burned up; the flames will not consume you." God will be with us through all the tough situations that we face. He will not leave our sides.

We have all faced difficult situations in our lifetimes. During these times, we need to turn to God and trust that he will bring us through them. James 1:2–3 says, "Dear brothers and sisters, when troubles of any kind come your way, consider it an opportunity for great joy. For you know that when your faith is tested, your endurance has a chance to grow." When you face tough situations, use it as a chance to grow. You will become a stronger person. Also, grow your relationship with God. Learning and growing are all a part of this beautiful life. This should bring you great joy! How can you learn and grow in your faith today?

DAY 14
Unique Gifts

We put our hope in the Lord. He is our help and our shield. In him our hearts rejoice, for we trust in his holy name. Let your unfailing love surround us, Lord, for our hope is in you alone.
—PSALM 33:20–22 (NLT)

On my life's journey, I have had a lot of hopes. I hoped to be a large animal veterinarian, but I changed my mind halfway through college. Then I hoped to be a pharmacist. I went through a year and a half of pharmacy school and then quit. Our plans don't always work out, but God knows our paths.

Don't give up hope because God has a plan for you. Keep your hope in God even when things don't go your way. Your way is not always the correct way, but God's way is correct. He knows best. What hopes did not come true for you? What hopes did come true for you? Psalm 139:14 says, "Thank you for making me so wonderfully complex! Your workmanship is marvelous—how well I know it."

God gave us the ability to make decisions. Sometimes we make the correct decisions, and sometimes we don't. When we don't make the correct decisions, God walks with us and guides us to the correct path. We are complex people. Each day, we can let our emotions get the best of us. Each day, God calls us to himself to help us through our many emotions. God made us, and his "workmanship is marvelous." God made each of us for a special purpose. He gave us unique gifts to share with others. Are you sharing your unique gifts with others?

DAY 15
Change

But those who trust in the Lord will find new strength.
They will soar high on wings like eagles. They will run
and not grow weary. They will walk and not faint.

—Isaiah 40:31 (NLT)

When my hopes didn't come true to become a veterinarian or pharmacist, I didn't give up. God had a new path for me. I had to get on the correct road. I now work in information technology and love it. My job allows me to be creative and challenged, all at the same time. God knew what my strengths were and guided me to the correct career path so that he could use those strengths each day.

If you feel like you are on the wrong path, move to a different path. You are feeling this for a reason. God is telling you to get on the correct path for you. Trust in God, and you will find new strength. When you got on the wrong path, how did you get on the correct one? Isaiah 12:2 says, "See, God has come to save me. I will trust in him and not be afraid. The Lord God is my strength and my song; he has given me victory." Choosing a career when you are eighteen years old is a tough decision. You think, *What is the best career for me? What am I good at? What doesn't feel like work?* These are all questions that we have asked ourselves.

When I was in middle school, I thought I wanted to be a computer programmer. I shadowed my uncle for a day, and I got to see what a computer programmer does. Then in high school, I changed my mind and decided that I wanted to be a large animal veterinarian. It is funny how my life's path took me back to information technology later in life. Now that I am forty-four years old, I often wonder about a degree in biblical studies. I am so fascinated with the Bible and trying to learn as much as I can about it. You see, as we age, we learn more and more about ourselves. We also realize that we are changing. Change is hard but a good thing in life. Change makes us grow into who we were meant to be. Change challenges us as well. How have you changed over the years?

DAY 16
Simple Moments

The Sovereign Lord will show his justice to the nations of the world. Everyone will praise him! His righteousness will be like a garden in early spring, with plants springing up everywhere.
—Isaiah 61:11 (NLT)

D o you take time to enjoy beautiful sunrises and sunsets, or do you walk right past them? God made sunrises and sunsets for you. He painted the sky for you. He also made all the pretty flowers and rainbows for you to enjoy. In summer, do you notice the butterflies? We should all take time to enjoy the gift of nature, stop and smell the flowers, and watch the sun rise and set. In autumn, we should enjoy the bright golds, oranges, and reds of the leaves. The leaves are so very beautiful. The snow is even beautiful, especially when it sticks to the trees. God paints a beautiful landscape. What beautiful landscapes of God have you noticed today?

Ecclesiastes 1:5 says, "The sun rises and the sun sets, then hurries around to rise again." The word that caught my attention in this verse was the word *hurries*. Our world is in a hurry. We hurry up and develop the next best thing, get to the next game, and buy the newest phone. It tells us to hurry here and hurry there. We shouldn't be in such a hurry all the time. We should take time and enjoy the moment. Enjoy life. Enjoy the slowness. Enjoy rest. Psalm 90:12 says, "Teach us to realize the brevity of life, so that we may grow in wisdom." Life is short, but we shouldn't be in such a hurry that we miss all the wonderful small moments of life. Take time to enjoy the small moments of life. Wake up early to enjoy the sunrise. Sit outside and watch the sunset. Stop and smell the flowers in your garden. Hug your family member a little longer. Take time to soak up all these simple moments of life. God wants you to notice these moments. How can you focus on these simple moments?

DAY 17
Being Different

The Lord is for me, so I will have no fear.
—Psalm 118:6 (NLT)

God is always watching out for us. Knowing this should cause us to have no fear. Yet we are still afraid. It is human nature to be afraid. When fear sneaks up on you, just think about God being there for you. God is there with you every step of the way. God provides each of us peace.

When I was in kindergarten, I wore a patch on my eye. I had a lazy eye. I was so afraid of what other kids would think of me. I was different compared to everyone else. I was unique. The kids were nice to me. They had lots of questions though. "Why do you have to wear that on your eye?" "How long do you have to wear it for?" "Does the patch make your eye hot?" Trying to make friends when you look different is hard. However, you shouldn't fear because God is for you. What challenging situation did you have while growing up? What challenging situation are you dealing with now? Psalm 91:5 says, "Do not be afraid of the terrors of the night, nor the arrow that flies in the day." I am very afraid of the dark, and I have always been since I was a child. We did barn chores late into the night. When my chores were done, I ran from the barn to the house. I always worried that a bear or wolf would attack me. God said, "Do not be afraid of the terrors of the night." Are you afraid of the dark or something else?

DAY 18
Fresh Start

The flowers are springing up, the season of singing birds has come,
and the cooing of turtledoves fills the air. The fig trees are forming
young fruit, and the fragrant grapevines are blossoming.
—Song of Songs 2:12–13 (NLT)

I love spring. I love all the flowers and the grass turning green.
Everything gets a fresh start. Sometimes I need a fresh start and a
new mindset. I have always been a goal planner. Each year, I come up
with four goals to focus on. For many years, it was reading the Bible.
Another goal was to start a disciplined exercise schedule. One other goal
was to write this book. The most common goal I have every year is to
improve my connections with others. If I am not careful, I can become
very isolated. I love to focus on my own tasks, which then puts stress on
my relationships. I need to schedule time with my family and friends to
help improve my connections throughout the year.

Does spring give you a fresh start and a new mindset? James 1:4
says, "So let it grow, for when your endurance is fully developed, you
will be perfect and complete, needing nothing." Every year, we can work
on something to improve ourselves. It could be learning something
new, training for a marathon, or working on our relationships with
God and our family members. Regardless of the goal you set, you will
become stronger in the end. Make sure each month you break down
your goals into small tasks. This will give you the motivation to keep
going. What goals do you want to set for this year? What goals are you
already working on?

DAY 19
Couch Days

Dear friend, I hope all is well with you and that you are as healthy in body as you are strong in spirit.
—3 JOHN 1:2 (NLT)

I thank God every day for my health. In my twenties, I was diagnosed with hepatitis C. It was a long, hard road to recovery. Every Friday night for one year, I had to inject myself in the stomach with special medication. The weekends ended up being what I labeled as couch days. The medication would make me so tired. The first round of treatment ended up not working, so I had to go through treatment again. This time, the treatment plan was simply taking a pill every day for three months. During this time, I thanked God for healing my liver. I knew God would heal me, and I am happy to report that I am healed from hepatitis C. Thank you, God, for healing me.

How is God healing you? First Corinthians 6:20 says, "For God bought you with a high price. So, you must honor God with your body." God is telling us that we must take care of our bodies. We need to take good care of ourselves physically and emotionally. We should exercise regularly, eat healthy food, and spend time with others to strengthen us emotionally.

If you had to give a rating of how well you take care of your body, 1 being poor and 10 being excellent, what rating would you give yourself? Currently, I rate myself at a 6. I need to eat better and drink more water. I also need to exercise more. I should get in ten thousand steps a day. I probably average three thousand steps. Looking at that number makes me disappointed in myself. I can do better, and I should do better because God gave me this one wonderful body. I need to take care of it if I want to live to be one hundred years old. How can you take better care of your body today? Set some good goals to help you achieve it.

DAY 20
Help Others

A cheerful heart is good medicine, but a broken spirit saps a person's strength.
—PROVERBS 17:22 (NLT)

Whenever I feel down, I like to have a conversation with my husband. He always cheers me up and helps me see the positive in my situation. "A cheerful heart is good medicine." Who cheers you up? Whoever that is, make sure to schedule weekly or monthly get-togethers with him or her. Having a positive person in your life is necessary for good mental health. As with any relationship, you need to spend time face-to-face with that person on a regular basis. It should be a time with no distractions, no phones, and just sitting and listening. How can you schedule more time with that person who cheers you up? How can you spend more quiet time with God?

First Thessalonians 4:1 says, "Finally, dear brothers and sisters, we urge you in the name of the Lord Jesus to live in a way that pleases God, as we have taught you. You live this way already, and we encourage you to do so even more." Every day, we should spend quiet time with God in prayer and thanksgiving. We should also live in a way that pleases God. One way that we can do this is using our gifts to help others. God gave us these gifts so we can help each other out. How can you use your gifts to help others?

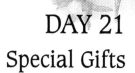

DAY 21
Special Gifts

God has given each of you a gift from his great variety of spiritual gifts. Use them well to serve one another.

—1 PETER 4:10 (NLT)

God gives us each our own special gifts and talents. We need to use those gifts and talents to help others. One of my special gifts is the gift of organization. I love organizing so much. It's like my own little hobby. I love to read books about organizing too. I love organizing our house and my children's rooms. I also love organizing my to-do list at work.

What is your own special gift? How are you using it for God and others? Galatians 6:10 says, "Therefore, whenever we have the opportunity, we should do good to everyone—especially to those in the family of faith." My children and I volunteer at our church's food pantry every month. Our job is packaging up the toiletries. Each bag has two rolls of toilet paper, a bar of soap, toothpaste, Kleenex, shampoo, and sometimes a miscellaneous item. Packaging these items up for the less fortunate makes me realize how blessed we are. People deserve good lives even when they are going through a tough financial time. I am glad that my children and I can help the less fortunate out during their time of need. Do you have a food pantry in your area where you can volunteer? If not, how can you help the less fortunate?

DAY 22
Crossroads

*Trust in the Lord with all your heart; do not depend
on your own understanding. Seek his will in all you
do, and he will show you which path to take.*

—Proverbs 3:5–6 (NLT)

When you get lost, look to God for help in finding the correct
path to take. Seek his will always. When I was in pharmacy
school back in the early 2000s, I felt lost. I felt like I was not where I
was supposed to be. I made a hard decision to leave pharmacy school
during my second year. I walked away without a plan. I knew God
would take care of me during this time. I ended up going to a job fair at
a local insurance company and walked out with a job that day. I worked
for the insurance company for a year and then at a health-care facility.
God, you are so good.

How has God helped you find your correct path in life? When you
are lost, do you consult God on what to do? God will listen to and guide
you to the correct path. Talk to God about the path options you have
and listen to what he says. His answer may surprise you. If you are at a
crossroads today, talk to God about it.

DAY 23
Spread the Bible

For God is working in you, giving you the desire and the power to do what pleases him. Do everything without complaining or arguing.
—Philippians 2:13–14 (NLT)

God tells us to do everything without complaining or arguing. I have to say that I complain and argue a lot. I need to work on both. I argue because I always want to be right. I complain because I want things to be perfect. Being right and perfect should not be my focus in life. It should not be your focus in life either. Loving and helping others should be our focus in life. God gave you a great purpose to do good work in this world.

How can you stop complaining and be grateful for the many blessings you have in your life? First Timothy 2:15 says, "Work hard so you can present yourself to God and receive his approval. Be a good worker, one who does not need to be ashamed and who correctly explains the word of truth." We should be good workers every day. We should do our best at our jobs. We should help others throughout the day. We should also spread the truth of the Bible to everyone we meet. This is part of our mission. Do you feel comfortable spreading the truth of the Bible to others? If you don't feel comfortable, how can you become comfortable with it? I challenge you to spread the Bible to one person this month—just one. You can do this!

DAY 24
Hard Things

For I can do everything through Christ, who gives me strength.
—Philippians 4:13 (NLT)

I can do hard things. God will help me. In 2006, I had major surgery: a right hemicolectomy. Six inches of my colon was taken out because I had a benign tumor. I was in the hospital for eight days. During those days, I could not eat or drink. It was tough. I was in a lot of pain. I was lucky to have God in my life, who gave me strength during that difficult time.

Has God brought you through a tough time in your life? Reflect on that time. Psalm 18:1–2 says, "I love you, Lord; you are my strength. The Lord is my rock, my fortress, and my savior; my God is my rock, in whom I find protection. He is my shield, the power that saves me, and my place of safety." Writing a book is hard. This is my first book, and I have been very challenged by it. There were times when I wouldn't open my computer because I was so frustrated by my lack of words to put in my manuscript. However, God is giving me strength to keep going. God is encouraging me to keep typing these words. I am writing this book for God. I want others to experience his peaceful reminders. What hard things are you working on? Do you get frustrated? Do you feel like giving up? I am here to say keep going and don't give up. You are doing your purpose in life. Do it well.

DAY 25
Working for the Lord

Work hard so you can present yourself to God and receive his approval. Be a good worker, one who does not need to be ashamed and who correctly explains the word of truth.

—2 Timothy 2:15 (NLT)

God, help us to be hard workers. Help us to be good workers who are constantly helping others. Help us to do good and honest work every day.

The summer before I started college, I worked three jobs. I worked at a tree farm for the first part of the day and then in the deli of my local grocery store. On Friday nights, I was a waitress at our local steakhouse. All three jobs taught me how to work hard and be a good worker. I also grew up on a dairy farm, where I really learned to work.

Being a good worker is a gift from God. Give thanks to God for the wonderful gift he has given you. How can you work hard for God? Romans 12:11 says, "Never be lazy, but work hard and serve the Lord enthusiastically." I am a mom, which is another full-time job and the most challenging one I have. Being a mom is the most important job I have. Being able to take care of my family is a gift, and I am very grateful. The next time I am completely exhausted, I need to remind myself that I am working for the Lord and that I should serve him enthusiastically. Are you serving the Lord enthusiastically, or are you barely surviving each day? Spend some quiet time with God regarding this.

DAY 26
Be Kind

If your gift is to encourage others, be encouraging. If it is giving, give generously. If God has given you leadership ability, take the responsibility seriously. And if you have a gift of showing kindness to others, do it gladly.

—ROMANS 12:8 (NLT)

I asked my husband what my gift from God was. He said that it was kindness. When I looked up the meaning of kindness, it said, "The quality of being friendly, generous, and considerate." (1) I try to do all those things each day.

What is your gift from God? Psalm 145:17 says, "The Lord is righteous in everything he does; he is filled with kindness." God wants us to be kind to others. When you are having a bad day, are you kind to others? When you are impatient, are you kind to others? When you are angry with someone close to you, are you kind to others? When you are stressed out, are you kind to others? In all these situations, we have to remember to be kind to others. How can you be kind to others today?

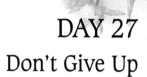

DAY 27
Don't Give Up

So let's not get tired of doing what is good. At just the right time we will reap a harvest of blessing if we don't give up. Therefore, whenever we have the opportunity, we should do good to everyone—especially to those in the family of faith.

—GALATIANS 6:9–10 (NLT)

God says we will "reap a harvest of blessing if we don't give up." When things get hard, do you give up? When things get hard, I am tempted to give up. I remember that doing my homework as a child was hard. I wanted to give up because I was so frustrated. I was thankful that my mom helped me with my homework when I was struggling. We grow the most when things are hard.

When you have an opportunity, make sure that you do good to everyone. Take advantage of every opportunity you get. Rejoice in the learning and growing you will go through with each opportunity. What good can you do today? Luke 18:1 says, "One day Jesus told his disciples a story to show that they should always pray and never give up."

Many times when we were house hunting, I wanted to give up. We drove around looking at house after house, but nothing seemed like the one. One day, my husband and his brother were taking a load of garbage to the dump, and they saw a for-sale sign next to this house on a quiet road. Mike and I did a walkthrough of the house shortly after that. When I first stepped inside, I knew that it was the one. We have been in our house for almost ten years, and we love it. Listen to God and never give up. What situation did you want to give up on? How did you overcome it?

DAY 28
Together

Two people are better off than one, for they can help each other succeed. If one person falls, the other can reach out and help.
—Ecclesiastes 4:9–10 (NLT)

One of the happiest days of my life was when I married my husband. Two people became one. We help each other often. We each have our strengths and our weaknesses. We complement each other well. I feel so blessed to have my husband. He is my best friend.

Who is the person in your life who helps you succeed? Colossians 3:15 says, "And let the peace that comes from Christ rule in your hearts. For as members of one body, you are called to live in peace. And always be thankful." I am very grateful for my little family. Children are a gift from God. Mike and I were blessed with two kids. I love my little family with my whole heart.

Romans 15:2 says, "We should help others do what is right and build them up in the Lord." As a family, we are always doing projects around the house. We work as a team to get things done. This morning, we worked on cleaning up our basement. We spent a couple of hours decluttering and getting rid of things that we no longer needed. Mike ended up building some shelves to store our son's toy farm set. We still have many more shelves to build so that we can continue to organize the space. Together, we made progress by helping each other out. We are hoping that this summer, we will redo the landscaping around our house. That will be a huge project, but as a team of four, we will get it done. Does your family work on projects together?

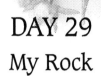

DAY 29
My Rock

My victory and honor come from God alone. He is my
refuge, a rock where no enemy can reach me.
—Psalm 62:7 (NLT)

Having a relationship with God is the most important relationship you will have in your life. You should talk to God throughout the day. God wants a relationship with you. He wants to hear from you. He wants you to tell him all your thoughts, fears, worries, and dreams. He wants to know all about you. God is marvelous. What do you want to talk to God about today? Psalm 71:3 says, "Be my rock of safety where I can always hide. Give the order to save me, for you are my rock and my fortress."

Do you know that not going to church is a sin? I didn't know this until I was well into my adult years. There are only fifty-two Sundays in a year, and God deserves our time and attention. The main point for going to church is to get the Eucharist. Every time I get communion, I get to take in the body and blood of Jesus. What a gift! Do you go to church on a weekly basis? Why or why not? Sometimes I hear people say that they don't get anything out of church. I prepare for mass every week. I have a mass journal that has all the Sunday readings in it, and I read them on Saturdays. Then while in church as the priest or deacon is giving the homily, I take notes in my mass journal. I ask myself how God is speaking to me that week and what he is trying to tell me. If we want to get something out of going to church, we need to put in the effort. We need to pray about it as well. If you haven't been to church in a while, I encourage you to go next Sunday. God will be so happy to see you.

DAY 30
Encourage Others

So encourage each other and build each other
up, just as you are already doing.
—1 Thessalonians 5:11 (NLT)

During your day-to-day activities, make sure you are encouraging others. Be a bucket filler and not a bucket emptier. Give compliments to the people around you. Congratulate your children when they succeed at something new. Smile at complete strangers to make their day. This little act of kindness can cheer up someone who is having a bad day. I love it when people spread joy around the world. Our world needs more joy. Spread joy around like confetti. Don't hold back. How have you spread joy today?

Jude 1:20–21 says, "But you, dear friends, must build each other up in your most holy faith, pray in the power of the Holy Spirit, and await the mercy of our Lord Jesus Christ, who will bring you eternal life. In this way, you will keep yourselves safe in God's love." I love to schedule friend get-togethers throughout the year. Ideally, I wish we could meet every month, but we all have very busy lives. Sometimes we get together over dinner, or we hang out at someone's house. One time, we checked out a new grocery store together. Regardless of where we hang out, we always have great conversations. I enjoy this time so very much. We were meant to have close friends in our lives to help us "build each other up." Who are your close friends? Have you seen them lately? If not, send them a text and get together soon.

DAY 31
Forgive Others

*Since God chose you to be the holy people he loves, you must
clothe yourselves with tenderhearted mercy, kindness, humility,
gentleness, and patience. Make allowance for each other's faults
and forgive anyone who offends you. Remember, the Lord forgave
you, so you must forgive others. Above all, clothe yourselves
with love, which binds us all together in perfect harmony.*

—COLOSSIANS 3:12–14 (NLT)

Everyone has faults. Please forgive anyone who offends you.
Remember that to be forgiven by God, you must also forgive others.
You cannot hold a grudge and expect to be forgiven of your sins. Above
all, love others well. Try to do your best every day. That's all God asks
of you.

There have been many situations in my life when I needed to forgive
others. It wasn't easy to do, but it was necessary. I am guessing you can
think of situations where you had to forgive others too. Even when our
feelings are hurt badly, we still forgive the other person. Everyone has
faults. We ourselves have faults. Let's do the right thing and forgive. Do
you have someone in your life you need to forgive? Matthew 6:14 says,
"If you forgive those who sin against you, your heavenly Father will
forgive you." It is important to forgive others so that God can forgive
you of your sins.

DAY 32
Patience

Always be humble and gentle. Be patient with each other, making allowance for each other's faults because of your love. Make every effort to keep yourselves united in the Spirit, binding yourselves together with peace.
—Ephesians 4:2–3 (NLT)

Raising children requires a lot of patience, especially in the beginning. I remember the sleepless nights and the never-ending diaper changes. Each day was a test of my patience; however, I was so tired that my patience ran thin quickly. My children required a lot of my attention. As my children got older, it got easier. They started doing things for themselves like brushing their teeth and combing their hair. I can't believe how fast the years have gone. We only have five summers left with our oldest and seven with our youngest. I need to cherish the rest of our days together. When my kids move out of our house, I am going to be heartbroken. I love having my kids in my home. I love giving them hugs every night before bed. I love hearing their stories each day. I love playing cards and board games with them. Was your patience ever tested during a phase of your life? How did you deal with it?

DAY 33
Prayers

For everyone who asks, receives. Everyone who seeks, finds.
And to everyone who knocks, the door will be opened.
—Matthew 7:8 (NLT)

Prayers do come true. God is always listening. One thing that I always pray for is patience. I ask God for patience all the time. I want things to happen fast, but that doesn't always happen. I prayed for three years to get a job at church. During this time, I had to be patient, and it was super hard. I wanted that job immediately, but God had another plan. God's plan is always correct. He knows best. I did get the job at church, and I worked there for a little over a year. I also prayed that God would heal my hepatitis C. It took a few years of praying, but I am cured of it. God is good. I prayed for a family of my own for many years, and I am grateful for my little family of four. God listens, but it is on his own time line and not ours. What is one thing you have been praying for?

DAY 34
Serve God

No one can serve two masters. For you will hate one and love the other; you will be devoted to one and despise the other. You cannot serve God and be enslaved to money.
—Matthew 6:24 (NLT)

This verse hits me right in the gut. Our world tells us to make as much money as we can so that we can have a good life and retirement. It says, "Work hard to make more money." But the more money we make, the more money we spend. Money should not be the most important thing in life. God should be the most important in life. We need to serve God instead of being enslaved to money. We should focus on God and not on money. Let's use our money to help others.

For Christmas last year, we participated in the box-of-joy, gift-giving event at our church. We picked up a shoebox and decided to shop for a needy seven-year-old girl. We picked out many items to put into the shoebox. Our shoebox was shipped overseas to her. It felt good to use our money to help this girl.

How can you better serve God and others today? Hebrews 13:5 says, "Don't love money; be satisfied with what you have. For God has said, 'I will never fail you. I will never abandon you.'" We need to be satisfied with what we have. Everything we have is from God, and God knows what we need before we even know what we need. God is our Master. We should respect him.

DAY 35
Loneliness

Our people must learn to do good by meeting the urgent needs of others; then they will not be unproductive.
—TITUS 3:14 (NLT)

I work from home now, but when I used to work in the office, my coworkers and I used to have lunch together one day a week. A few of us would pick up food for everyone in the office. Then we would all sit down together and have lunch. We learned so much about each other by doing this. It was a great time to connect with one another. It was a time to laugh and have fun together. I miss my coworkers and those days. Ever since COVID-19, I have been working from home full-time. I have come to realize that I am a homebody. I love being at home, and I hardly ever get out of the house. I even put off going to the grocery store as long as possible because I want to stay home.

Lately though, I feel lonely because I am so isolated. I miss my coworkers and friends. I miss having great conversations. I miss laughing and smiling. To combat my loneliness, I want to start a Bible study at my church. I think it would be good for me to get out and interact with a group of people in person again. My close coworkers and I try to have lunch once a month. When we get together, we enjoy great food and conversations. It's nice to see each other in person. Have you ever struggled with loneliness in your life? How did you deal with it?

DAY 36
Bible Reading

All Scripture is inspired by God and is useful to teach us what is true and to make us realize what is wrong in our lives. It corrects us when we are wrong and teaches us to do what is right.
—2 Timothy 3:16–17 (NLT)

I will never forget the day in second grade when my name was written on the board. I was talking to my friend while my teacher was trying to teach. He gave me many warning glares before he wrote my name on the board, but I ignored all of them. I was quiet after he wrote my name up there.

God always encourages us to do what is right, but sometimes we mess up and do the wrong thing. The Bible "corrects us when we are wrong and teaches us to do what is right." I enjoy reading the Bible every night, and I learn something every day. Every night, I read the Catholic daily mass readings and then do a Bible study. Currently, I am studying the book of James. By doing these Bible studies, I am learning so much. The questions it asks make me think about what I have read. Do you read the Bible on a regular basis? Why or why not?

DAY 37
Routine

*As soon as I pray, you answer me; you
encourage me by giving me strength.*
—Psalm 138:3 (NLT)

*T*hank you, God, for listening to my prayers. I love your encouragement;
it gives me strength for the next day. I pray before bed every night.
I have been doing this every night since I was in the fourth grade. I
remember my grandma teaching me how to pray before bed. Praying
gives me peace at the end of a busy day. It helps me take a step back
and look at all the blessings that I have. *Thank you, God, for everything
you have given me.* Prayer is a regular part of my day. I wish I could
do Pilates as a regular part of my day. I struggle with it every week.
I average about three-to-four times a week. This week, I fell off the
Pilates wagon. I haven't done it at all this week. Why can't my Pilates
routine be like my prayer routine? I should ask God for help with my
Pilates routine. I clearly can't do it by myself. Do you ever struggle with
a routine and sticking with it? Pray to God about it and ask him to help
you. He is always listening and willing to help.

DAY 38
Bed Rest and Smartphones

Then Jesus said, "Come to me, all of you who are weary
and carry heavy burdens, and I will give you rest."
—Matthew 11:28 (NLT)

With both of my pregnancies, I was placed on bed rest. With my oldest, I was on bed rest for one week. With my youngest, I was on bed rest for three weeks. I suffered from preeclampsia (high blood pressure during pregnancy). Both of my children were born at thirty-seven weeks. During my bed rest, I did a lot of planning. With my oldest, I made my meal plan for three months. I read many books and took a lot of naps. I also watched a lot of television.

Jesus promises us that he will give us rest. All we must do is ask him for help. Do you ever feel overwhelmed because of your smartphone? I do. All the alerts and notifications are exhausting. Every few months, I go through my phone and mute as many notifications as I can, but it is still overwhelming. It's sad how addicted we are to our phones. If someone had told me thirty years ago that I was going to be addicted to my phone, I wouldn't have believed them. For Lent one year, I gave up social media, and it was the best thing I ever did. I am no longer addicted to social media. Do I still go on social media? I do, but the time I spend on it is much less than it was. Do you have any addictions that you need help with? Ask God for help.

DAY 39
Good Works

*If you are wise and understand God's ways, prove it
by living an honorable life, doing good works with
the humility that comes from wisdom.*
—James 3:13 (NLT)

Today, I studied in the book of James, and the topic was about having true faith. True faith is having faith but also good works. When I was in college, I helped my husband's family with an Easter egg hunt for disabled children. We hid all the eggs in the park. It was a joy seeing all their smiles as they found the eggs. Their Easter baskets were overflowing with eggs. We enjoyed doing this every year. Helping others brings joy to my heart. I feel good that I can use my time and talents to help others who can't always help themselves. Who needs your help?

DAY 40
Pet Rabbits

All praise to God, the Father of our Lord Jesus Christ. God is our merciful Father and the source of all comfort. He comforts us in all our troubles so that we can comfort others. When they are troubled, we will be able to give them the same comfort God has given us.
—2 CORINTHIANS 1:3–4 (NLT)

G od is our Father. He is our comfort in this world. I feel so blessed to have his peace and comfort in my life.

When I was a child, I had seven pet rabbits. I loved taking care of them and taking them to the county fair in the summer. However, our dog ended up getting into the barn where the rabbits lived, and all my rabbits ended up dying. It was one of the hardest things to go through. Some of my rabbits were prizewinning rabbits. I knew that I could turn to God during this difficult time and that he would bring me comfort. Thank you, God, for providing comfort during hardships.

Think of a hardship you had to go through. How did God help you through it? Also, when I think of comfort, I think of camping. Our family enjoys going camping every summer. We love to rent a cabin and always bring our golf cart with us. We enjoy relaxing by the pool, cooking food over the fire, and spending time with one another. It's a time when we unwind and relax. Do you have an activity that brings you comfort?

DAY 41
Enjoy Life

Devote yourselves to prayer with an alert mind and a thankful heart.
—Colossians 4:2 (NLT)

When you pray, be alert. Think about what you are saying to God. Don't become a robot and say the same things repeatedly. I need to work on that. I repeat myself a lot in my prayers at night. I need to focus on having a conversation with God. Pray to God and then listen to his answer. Don't keep talking. You need to stop and listen to him during your prayers. Again, it's another thing I need to work on.

When you pray, also have a thankful heart. Thank God for the wonderful day you had. If it is morning, thank God for allowing you to wake up to another day. Each day is a gift from God. Enjoy it. Enjoy life. Life is short, so be thankful for each day you get on this earth.

One way we like to enjoy life is going out to eat with my mom. The kids and I go out to eat with her. Sometimes we do a little shopping in our local shops. After that, we go back home and enjoy an afternoon of board and card games. I am always so thankful to be able to spend time with my mom. How do you like to enjoy life?

DAY 42
Trials

I have told you all of this so that you may have peace in me. Here on earth you will have many trials and sorrows. But take heart, because I have overcome the world.
—John 16:33 (NLT)

On Earth, we will have many trials and sorrows. One of our greatest trials right now is the fight against COVID-19. This illness is killing so many people. This illness is also causing families to go their separate ways based on vaccination status. Some people agree with vaccination, and some people don't. The same debate happens with masking. Some believe that masking works, and some don't. I wish COVID-19 would disappear, but I think it's here to stay. We are always going to have to deal with it.

Another trial that I had was a summer internship in college. Part of this internship was helping milk cows at one of the participating farms. While I was there, a cow ended up kicking me. I fell over, and the cow stepped on my back. I also sprained my ankle. Everything turned out OK, but it was a rough few weeks. Even though we have trials on Earth, we should take heart because God has overcome the world. What trials and sorrows have you gone through?

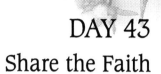

DAY 43
Share the Faith

*Fight the good fight for the true faith. Hold tightly to
the eternal life to which God has called you, which you
have declared so well before many witnesses.*

—1 TIMOTHY 6:12 (NLT)

D o you share your faith with others? If you don't, why not? Are you
worried about what others will think of you? Are you scared to
talk about Jesus to others? Do you feel uncomfortable in your faith? God
wants you to spread the good news.

At the end of mass, the deacon always says, "Go forth and spread
the good news." Every day we should be sharing our faith with others.
We should guide people to Jesus. It is our duty to do these things. God
will be so happy! God loves a faithful servant.

My son spreads the good news often. He has a friend who doesn't
believe in God. He told me that he is trying to get that friend to believe
in God. If my son hears anyone misusing God's name, he reminds that
person not to take the Lord our God's name in vain. When classmates
of his are picking on one another, he encourages them to know the
Lord. My son is always thinking about spreading the good news. First
Corinthians 9:23 says, "I do everything to spread the Good News and
share in its blessings." How can you spread the good news to others
today?

DAY 44
Praying For Others

Confess your sins to each other and pray for each other so that you may be healed. The earnest prayer of a righteous person has great power and produces wonderful results.
—James 5:16 (NLT)

I pray for others nightly. Currently, I am praying for twenty-three people. Some people are very sick, and some people are healthy. Most of the people I pray for don't know that I am doing it. Sometimes I pray for all the people in the hospital too. I believe that prayers are powerful and that they do work. Ephesians 6:18 says, "Pray in the Spirit at all times and on every occasion. Stay alert and be persistent in your prayers for all believers everywhere." I have prayed for many jobs and my health. I have prayed for my community. I have prayed for my goals. I have prayed for understanding and patience. I have prayed for my children and my husband. I have prayed for so many things in my life. Did all my prayers come true? I would say that most of my prayers came true—the ones that aligned with God's plan. What do you pray for?

DAY 45
Practice Hospitality

When God's people are in need, be ready to help them. Always be eager to practice hospitality.
—Romans 12:13 (NLT)

Every New Year's Eve, our friends got together. We alternated hosting every year as well. Each of us brought a snack and some beverages to share. We enjoyed card games for hours. We rang in the New Year together. Then we played cards into the early hours of the morning. Those were the best years. I miss them so much. We no longer get together on New Year's Eve. We have our own families, children, and responsibilities. Honestly, I thought our New Year's Eve parties would go on through the entirety of our lives. It makes me sad that we no longer get together. But as we know, life always changes. My little family started a new tradition for New Year's Eve. I make a charcuterie board. Then we play darts. It's a night of snacking and competition. Do you practice hospitality in your life?

DAY 46
Comfort

Even when I walk through the darkest valley, I will not be afraid, for you are close beside me. Your rod and your staff protect and comfort me.
—PSALM 23:4 (NLT)

When the COVID-19 pandemic hit, we needed some comfort in our life. Watching episodes of *Little House on the Prairie* was our comfort. During the pandemic, everything was super stressful. I was working from home. We had meeting after meeting about COVID-19. On top of that, both of my children were doing virtual school from home. It was the most stressed I have ever been. I tried to be a coworker, mom, lunch lady, and teacher all at once. It was hard on all of us. So each night, we would sit down as a family and watch a *Little House* episode. It took us six months to get through all the seasons of the show. Watching a show about simpler times helped make our worries go away for an hour. It was an hour of peace and comfort. I looked forward to this peaceful hour every day. What was your comfort during the pandemic?

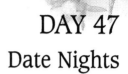

DAY 47
Date Nights

Since they are no longer two but one, let no one
split apart what God has joined together.
—Matthew 19:6 (NLT)

My husband and I enjoy going out on date nights once a month. It's a night of great conversation and food. We get to have a conversation without any interruptions from our children. It's a time to unwind from the long workweek and just have fun.

Do you go on date nights with your spouse? I highly encourage you to do this if you don't. It is important and necessary in any marriage. As you know, marriage requires a lot of communication, and date nights provide the perfect platform for great conversations between your spouse and yourself. Another great thing to do is going on vacation with just your spouse. My husband and I went to Mexico for a week. It was great to get away from our daily responsibilities and just relax with each other. Your marriage is just as important as your family life. Make sure to take time each month to keep your marriage thriving.

DAY 48
Game Nights and the Weather

Do everything without complaining and arguing.
—Philippians 2:14 (NLT)

As a family, we love to have family game nights. We love board games, card games, and playing darts. We love to get competitive. Whoever wins the game gets to pick the next game we play. Some nights we play several different games. When we are playing our games, we usually end up arguing with one another over the rules. One person thinks the rule means one thing, and someone else thinks it means something else. We end up getting out the rule book and discussing what it says. Someone usually ends up complaining, and it's usually me. I get frustrated over the rules of the games.

I feel that people complain often about the weather. When its summer, people complain that it's too hot outside. When its winter, people complain that it's too cold outside. When it's raining outside, people complain. When it's windy outside, people complain about that too. We should enjoy the seasons as they come. We should enjoy God's beauty. Do you complain or argue a lot? If so, have a nice long talk with God about it.

DAY 49
Hard Days

These trials will show that your faith is genuine. It is being tested as fire tests and purifies gold—though your faith is far more precious than mere gold. So when your faith remains strong through many trials, it will bring you much praise and glory and honor on the day when Jesus Christ is revealed to the whole world.

—1 PETER 1:7 (NLT)

A family member got in a terrible accident in mid-January of 2019. I remember waiting in the emergency department and hearing the helicopter he was in land on the roof. This day was the hardest and longest day of my life. I totally thought I had lost this family member. That day made me realize how short life can be. While in that emergency department, I prayed and prayed and prayed for him to live. I know that God heard me because my family member is here and alive and well. Thank you, God, for the gift of comfort that you provided me on that day and the weeks that followed. I needed all of it. Did God give you comfort on a hard day? Reflect on that hard day and give thanks to God.

DAY 50
Obsessive Hand Washing

For God is not a God of disorder but of peace, as in all the meetings of God's holy people.
—1 CORINTHIANS 14:33 (NLT)

When I was a child, I washed my hands endlessly. If I got a speck of dirt on my hand, I would wash my hands. I washed my hands so much that they became dry and bled. It was awful. I am not sure how I recovered from my obsessive-compulsive disorder.

Disorder disrupts the peace in our lives. A messy house disrupts my peace. Not having meals planned for the week disrupts my peace. Children fighting disrupts my peace. However, God is a God of peace. Whenever things get out of control in our world, we should turn to God to give us peace. He can calm us down and give us rest. Do you ever have disorder in your life? How do you deal with it?

DAY 51
Know Me

O Lord, you have examined my heart and know everything about me.
—Psalm 139:1 (NLT)

When I was young, I was extremely shy. I didn't talk to anyone. I was more of a listener than a speaker. As I grew up, talking became easier to do. I enjoyed telling stories to my friends and participating more in school. As an adult, I enjoy talking to others. I love asking questions and learning about others. For work a few years back, we did a personality colors' test, and my colors were gold and orange. Gold traits are loyalty, respects rules, responsible, and organized. Orange traits are adventurous, competitive, and impulsive. I love making lists, organizing my house, and learning new things. Now that I work from home, I feel like my personality is changing. I have become a homebody and enjoy being by myself.

God knows everything about us. He made us. Matthew 10:30 says, "And the very hairs on your head are all numbered." God knows what is going to happen to you today and everything that will happen to you in the future. Psalm 126:3 says, "Yes, the Lord has done amazing things for us! What joy!"

God, thank you for giving me all my personality traits. Thank you for making me unique. Thank you for all my special gifts. Some days, I feel like I don't deserve all these special gifts, but then I remember that you love me and always will. For that, I am grateful.

Do you like all the personality traits that God has given you? How can you give thanks to God today?

DAY 52
God Is in Control

God blesses those who patiently endure testing and temptation. Afterward they will receive the crown of life that God has promised to those who love him.

—James 1:12 (NLT)

I wish I could always be in control. I wish my house was always clean, our meals were always planned, and I could keep everything together. However, life doesn't always mean that everything is perfect. We endure testing and temptation. We endure trials and suffering, but God is always in control. God knows everything that will happen, and he will make sure his plan takes place. God will do what is best for us even when we think our plan is better. Trust God. God is in control.

Romans 8:6 says, "So letting your sinful nature control your mind leads to death. But letting the Spirit control your mind leads to life and peace." We will have more peace in our lives if we let God control them instead of us trying to control everything. I know that for many of us, this will be very hard to let go of. We need to trust in God's plan for our lives. He knows best. Remember, he knows everything about us. Ask God what he wants you to do and then listen to him.

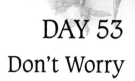

DAY 53
Don't Worry

Worry weighs a person down; an encouraging word cheers a person up.
—Proverbs 12:25 (NLT)

D o you worry a lot? Worry wears you down. When you find yourself worrying, pray to God. God can take the weight of your worries.

When I was a child, I would worry all the time. I remember my grandma telling me, "If you worry too much, you will get an ulcer." When I was in college, I worried constantly about my grades. I wanted to earn straight As in every class. I studied all the time, but then I also worried all the time. I worried so much that I ended up with a stomach ulcer. I took medicine for three months to cure it. Now when I worry, I remind myself of that ulcer and then let the worry go.

Matthew 6:31–33 says, "So, don't worry about these things ... these things dominate the thoughts of unbelievers, but your heavenly Father already knows all your needs. Seek the Kingdom of God above all else, and live righteously, and he will give you everything you need." God is always watching out for us. He knows what we need before we know what we need. This is God's peaceful reminder: Do not worry.

DAY 54
Love Others Well

So now I am giving you a new commandment: Love each other.
Just as I have loved you, you should love each other. Your love for
one another will prove to the world that you are my disciples.
—John 13:34–35 (NLT)

The Bible tells us loud and clear to love one another. Tell others that you love them. Hug them. Kiss them. Even when you have a disagreement, clothe yourself with love. Love brings us closer together. Love brings us closer to God. Love comes from God, and God is love. Love your children well by spending time with them. Love your husband well by going on weekly or monthly date nights. Love your parents by taking care of them. Love your friends by spending time with them on a regular basis. We should also love our enemies and complete strangers. We should love everyone.

On Valentine's Day, many love to express their love for each other, but we should express our love each day. First Corinthians 13:4–5 and 7 says, "Love is patient and kind. Love is not jealous or boastful or proud or rude …Love never gives up, never loses faith, is always hopeful, and endures through every circumstance." First Corinthians 16:14 says, "And do everything with love."

DAY 55
Founder's Day

One day as he saw the crowds gathering, Jesus went up on the mountainside and sat down. His disciples gathered around him, and he began to teach them.

—MATTHEW 5:1–2 (NLT)

E very September, we celebrate our town's Founder's Day. It is a day of crafts and treats. The streets are filled with craft vendors. I love going every year. I usually find something decorative for my house. We always stop by the candy booth to buy a caramel apple. I usually hate crowds, but I make an exception for this yearly tradition.

In the above verse, Jesus decided to teach his disciples. He taught them about the beatitudes, which are part of the Sermon on the Mount. Jesus taught them everything he knew. Read Matthew chapters 5, 6, and 7, which go over Jesus's teachings. What did you learn? Is there an area in your life you need to work on?

DAY 56
Do Not Be Afraid

Don't be afraid, for I am with you. Don't be discouraged,
for I am your God. I will strengthen you and help you.
I will hold you up with my victorious right hand.
—Isaiah 41:10 (NLT)

The Bible says, "Do not be afraid," 365 times. It's our reminder to live fearlessly every day. All of us go through times of fear. When you are afraid, put your trust in God. He won't fail or abandon you. Pray to the Lord and have no fear.

When I was first diagnosed with hepatitis C, I was so afraid that I was going to die. I cried many tears. I remember the day I was diagnosed; I had been visiting friends. I cried the whole night. I was worried that I had given this disease to my husband. I had so many emotions. My husband was tested and was negative. It took several years of treatment before I was healed.

God said, "Don't be discouraged. I will strengthen you and help you." Listen to God. He will take care of you. What are you currently afraid of? What are you struggling with? Whatever it is, give it all to God.

DAY 57
Photo Nature Challenge

The Lord is my shepherd; I have all that I need. He lets me rest in green meadows; he leads me beside peaceful streams. He renews my strength. He guides me along right paths, bringing honor to his name.

—PSALM 23:1–3 (NLT)

Take time each day to enjoy nature. Enjoy the sunrise with its vibrant colors. Take time to smell the flowers. Enjoy the beauty of the mountains and waterfalls. Admire the sunset and thank God for another awesome day. Enjoy all of God's wonderful works. He created them all for you.

One thing I am thinking of doing is a photo nature challenge. This challenge would be to take one photo of nature each day. Let's do it for a month and then admire all the wonderful photos we took. Are you in?

DAY 58
God's Gifts

Commit your actions to the Lord, and your plans will succeed.
—Proverbs 16:3 (NLT)

I have wanted to write this book for over ten years. Every year, I make a goal to write it, but then I never start it. This is the year that I decided to fulfill that goal. I am dedicating this book to God. His gifts are amazing and wonderful. We should not take any of these gifts for granted. Do you have a goal that you keep putting off? What is holding you back? Why don't you start right now?

DAY 59
Disney World

You can pray for anything, and if you have faith, you will receive it.
—Matthew 21:22 (NLT)

I have had many prayers answered by God. I prayed to have a husband, to go to the college of my choice, to be healed of hepatitis C, to have 2 children, and to get my current job role and dream house. God listened to my prayers. I had faith that these prayers would come true. I had also always wanted to go to Disney World, and I was able to go when I was twelve years old. My grandparents took me and my brother. We had an amazing time. Do you know what I remember about the trip? I remember swimming in the pools at the hotels. Epcot was great, but it was the small moments that I remember most. We drove from Wisconsin to Florida. It took us a few days, but the best part was spending time with my grandparents. My grandpa is no longer on this earth, and I miss him so much.

Making memories is what we should cherish while we are here. Enjoy all the small moments of your day. Enjoy time with family and friends. Enjoy being alive and thank God for another day on this earth. What is one thing you are praying for today?

DAY 60
Oklahoma Trip

*I am leaving you with a gift—peace of mind and heart. And the peace
I give is a gift the world cannot give. So don't be troubled or afraid.*
—JOHN 14:27 (NLT)

Have you ever had a bad day? I think everyone occasionally has a bad day. Even if you feel your day is terrible, try to focus on the positives of the day. Pray to God for peace of mind and heart. Don't wish your days away. Each day allows us to make positive differences in people's lives. Each day allows us to chase our dreams. Each day allows us to work on our relationships with others. Enjoy each day, even the ones that don't go so well. Each day is a gift from God. Remember, if you live to be seventy years old, you only get 25,550 days. Make each day count!

One summer, we decided to go to Oklahoma for a girl's trip. My mom, my mother-in-law, my sister-in-law, and I went. We drove from Wisconsin to Oklahoma in one day. Our main reason for going to this state was to go to the Pioneer Woman's mercantile store. We enjoyed breakfast and lunch there. We also enjoyed shopping at the store. That day was so peaceful. We just browsed and relaxed. It was a day to have fun with the girls. Do you ever take a girl's trip?

DAY 61
Go to Confession

Repent of your sins and turn to God, for the Kingdom of Heaven is near.
—MATTHEW 3:2 (NLT)

I am a Catholic. As Catholics, we are supposed to confess our sins in reconciliation every year. I am currently failing at this. It's been over three years since I went to reconciliation. Not going to reconciliation is another sin. I make up excuses so that I don't have to go: It's too far to drive, the time of reconciliation is inconvenient, or my sins aren't that bad. Going to reconciliation to repent of my sins is good for me and my relationship with God. It's necessary. Carrying all these sins around day after day is not good for me or you. God is willing to forgive us if we just ask him to.

I have been doing my prep work. I made a list of all my sins. Seeing it on paper made me realize all the areas I have done wrong in my life. I also realized that I have a lot of areas to improve on. I challenge you to write down all your sins. Then take the next step and go to confession.

DAY 62
Family Faith Formation Coordinator

Jesus looked at them intently and said, "Humanly speaking, it is impossible. But not with God. Everything is possible with God.
—Mark 10:27 (NLT)

I have always wanted to work for the church. I prayed for three years to have a church position open up. One day after a meeting with Deacon Todd, he pulled me aside and said that the church was developing a new position: family faith formation coordinator. He encouraged me to apply for it. After much thought, I decided to apply, even though I had a full-time job in information technology at a health-care facility. I told my husband that I was going to try working both jobs. He said that wasn't a good idea. I cried. I had prayed for this job, and it was suddenly available. I ended up taking the job and working two jobs for one year. I ultimately decided to step away from my family faith formation coordinator role. Working two jobs was exhausting, but I was so grateful that God created that job for me.

"Everything is possible with God." Even if you think there is no way, God will make a way. He is always listening to you. What is one thing you are asking God for?

DAY 63
Social Media Fast

Jesus replied, "The Scriptures say, 'You must worship the Lord your God and serve only him.'"
—Luke 4:8 (NLT)

Many years back, I realized that social media was consuming my time at night. I spent hours on it every night before bed. During Lent that year, I decided to fast from social media. It was the best forty days I ever had. During this time, I replaced social media with reading books. Reading brought me peace and got me away from my iPad screen. Eventually, I started reading the Bible every night. "Worship the Lord your God" and don't worship social media. Does social media consume your nights as well? Do you wish you could focus on some goals in your life? Try a social-media fast and focus on one goal. You will be amazed at what you can accomplish.

DAY 64
Mass Journal

*But those who do what is right come to the light so others
can see that they are doing what God wants.*
—JOHN 3:21 (NLT)

I recently bought a mass journal from Every Sacred Sunday. This
Catholic mass journal has all the Sunday readings in it for the entire
year. Every Saturday, I sit down with this journal. I go through all the
readings for that Sunday. This has been a game changer for me. I feel so
mentally prepared for mass. Also in this mass journal, there is a place
for homily notes. Taking notes in church has made me very engaged in
the mass. How is God speaking to me through the readings and homily?
When you go to church, bring a notebook and take notes during the
priest's homily. Also, if you are Catholic, check out this Catholic mass
journal on the internet. Search for Every Sacred Sunday.

DAY 65
Training a Steer

And he ordered us to preach everywhere and to testify that Jesus is the one appointed by God to be the judge of all—the living and the dead.
—Acts 10:42 (NLT)

When I was in middle school, I joined our local 4-H club. My main reason for joining was to show a steer at the county fair. Starting in March and ending in July, I spent hours training this steer. Training a steer taught me a lot of patience and responsibility. When the county fair came to town, I needed to show my steer. The judge would first judge the steer, and then I would be judged on how well I handled the animal. This was so stressful and scary. Animals don't always behave, even though you spend hours training them. I ended up having grand and reserve champion steers in back-to-back years. It was very rewarding.

God will be judging our lives. Have we been training well for it, or could we use some improvement? If you need improvement, start working on it today.

DAY 66
Sharing Your Talents

He will judge everyone according to what they have done.
—ROMANS 2:6 NLT

My husband is a very talented human being. He can fix anything. He was an electrician at one time. Many people ask for Mike's help, and Mike is always happy to help them out. Mike shares his talents with others well. His gift is the ability to fix anything and everything. He took our dryer apart twice and fixed it both times. He helped fix our son's four-wheeler. He has wired many houses and garages for others.

"He will judge everyone according to what they have done." I believe that God will be very happy with the work Mike has done for others. He has used his talents to help others, which is exactly why God gave him those talents. We shouldn't keep our talents all to ourselves. We should share our talents with others. What talent do you have? Have you shared your talent with others? Why or why not?

DAY 67
True Happiness

Three things will last forever—faith, hope, and love—and the greatest of these is love.
—1 CORINTHIANS 13:13 (NLT)

I have a sign in our bathroom that says, "Happiness=Faith, Hope, and Love." They are the three theological virtues. We believe in, trust in, and love God. All of these things will bring us happiness. Our world tries to tell us that new stuff or a family trip will bring us happiness. However, it's not true. Once the newness of your new stuff wears off, you will want more new stuff. Once your family trip is done, you will want to take another one. It's a vicious cycle. How do I know? I am guilty of buying new stuff all the time, and Amazon makes it too easy. My guilty pleasure is buying new books and highlighters. However, we should focus on God to make us happy. Believe in, trust in, and love God. How can you focus on God today? Take the first step.

For we must all stand before Christ to be judged. We will each receive whatever we deserve for the good or evil we have done in this earthly body.

—2 Corinthians 5:10 (NLT)

When I was in grade school, I struggled with schoolwork. Little did I know that I had ADHD. It was hard to pay attention to the teacher. When I took tests, I couldn't skip questions that I didn't answer. This caused me to fail tests. Math was extremely challenging, especially timed tests. I ended up getting special help on these tests. I remember when I finally got a 100 percent on one. It was a huge milestone for me. When I was in ninth grade, everything fell into place for me. I became an A student. I am so grateful to all my teachers for the extra help they gave me over the years. Thank you, Mrs. Wolf, for the extra help you gave me. Is there someone in your life who helped you through something difficult? Go and thank that person today.

DAY 69
Kindness

Instead, be kind to each other, tenderhearted, forgiving one another; just as God through Christ has forgiven you.
—Ephesians 4:32 (NLT)

I had a great group of friends in high school. However, there were many times when we picked on one another. We hurt one another's feelings often. In hindsight, we should have been kind to one another. About twenty years later, I wrote a letter to one of my friends and told her I was sorry for everything I had done to hurt her while we were in school. I still don't have a relationship with her, but I apologized to her. Is there anyone in your life that you need to apologize to? Do it today. Write that letter, make that call, or travel to go see that person.

DAY 70
Garden Rest

Then the way you live will always honor and please the Lord, and your lives will produce every kind of good fruit. All the while, you will grow as you learn to know God better and better.
—Colossians 1:10 (NLT)

The past several years, I have loved keeping a garden—well, several gardens. I have a vegetable and flower garden. I love seeing things grow and bloom. However, I hate all the work. I hate weeding, so we use landscape felt in between all the rows. Remembering to water it every night is daunting. I have decided that in 2023, I am not going to have any gardens—none. I need a break. I need a rest. It's OK to take a break. It's OK to rest. Exodus 23:10–11 says, "Plant and harvest your crops for six years, but let the land be renewed and lie uncultivated during the seventh year." Is there an area in your life where you need to rest and take a break? If so, do that.

DAY 71
Attachment

And may the Lord make your love for one another and for all people grow and overflow, just as our love for you overflows.
—1 Thessalonians 3:12 (NLT)

I get very attached to people. I don't deal well when people leave. People leave my current place of employment. It's hard on me. I always get so emotional. People leave big holes when they leave us, and it's hard to fill those holes back up. Sometimes that hole can't be filled. My grandma died in 1999, and it was hard on me. I still miss her so much. She lived across the road from us, so she came over to our house often. Whenever she came over, instead of knocking on the door, she would say, "Bang, bang." I can remember it vividly. I loved it when my grandma came over.

My friend Peggy retired from our place of work, and I miss her so much. We worked together for many years. Do you get attached to people too? What do you do to cope with the loss?

DAY 72
Hear the Call

So we keep on praying for you, asking our God to enable you to live a life worthy of his call. May he give you the power to accomplish all the good things your faith prompts you to do.
—2 Thessalonians 1:11 (NLT)

When my son was eight years old, he came to me, crying. I asked him why he was crying, and he said, "I think God wants me to be a priest." I asked him why he was crying about that, and he said, "I want to get married, and priests can't get married." In our Catholic faith, this is true. Priests cannot be married. To comfort my son, I told him that we should talk to Deacon Todd about why priests cannot be married. I gave him a great big hug.

I think about this conversation with my son often. He was hearing the call from God already. Being a priest may be his purpose in life. Our family goes to church every week. During mass, my son said all the priest's prayers. He knew them all by heart. At first, I was embarrassed that he was saying them out loud. I was afraid that everyone was looking at us. But as I looked around, people were smiling at him. He paid attention through the whole mass. I was proud of him. Do you know your call in life or yet? If you don't, ask God what your life's purpose is.

DAY 73
The Lesson We Teach

A servant of the Lord must not quarrel but must be kind to everyone, be able to teach, and be patient with difficult people.
—2 Timothy 2:24 (NLT)

Mike and I constantly teach our children to be kind to everyone, even if that person is not being kind to us. There will always be people who will challenge us. We need to be patient with them. We also teach our children to be bucket fillers instead of bucket emptiers. Mike and I want our children to be giving out compliments instead of cutting people down and to share a smile with a stranger. We want to spread joy wherever we go.

Psalm 116:5 says, "How kind the Lord is! How good he is! So merciful, this God of ours!" We need to be kind like God is kind. God's kindness is endless. In the gospel of Mark, there is a story of a woman who poured perfume over Jesus's head (See Mark 14:3). The story tells of the kindness this woman had for Jesus. She anointed his body for burial. Every day, let's focus on being kind to each other. If you have children, what lessons do you teach them? Do you practice what you preach?

DAY 74
Mid-Life Crisis

*So let us come boldly to the throne of our gracious
God. There we will receive his mercy, and we will
find grace to help us when we need it most.*
—Hebrews 4:16 (NLT)

I had a mid-life crisis when I was thirty-five years old. I debated on taking my own life, but do you know what stopped me? My family members flashed through my head, and I put the knife down. I couldn't leave them. They needed me, and I needed them. After this very dark day, I told myself that I would read the greatest self-help book around: the Bible. I started reading it every day. I badly needed God in my life. I knew that God would help me get out of the darkness and into the light.

The verse above says, "Let us come boldly to the throne of our gracious God … we will find grace to help us when we need it most." God helped me into the light, and for that, I am very grateful. Are you suffering right now? If so, seek help and seek God. God made you for a purpose, and you are important in his plan. He needs you. Your family needs you. Your friends need you. Your coworkers need you. You, my dear, are important in this world, and we love you. Step out of the darkness and into the light.

DAY 75
Just Ask

If you need wisdom, ask our generous God, and he will give it to you. He will not rebuke you for asking.
—JAMES 1:5 (NLT)

Do you ask God for what you want? I ask God, all the time, to help me understand the Bible. The Bible is a complicated book of books. In James, it says, "If you need wisdom, ask our generous God, and he will give it to you." Our God is indeed a very generous God. All we must do is ask him. Matthew 7:7 says, "Keep on asking, and you will receive what you ask for. Keep on seeking, and you will find. Keep on knocking, and the door will be opened to you." This is talking about prayer, specifically effective prayer.

Is prayer a regular part of your life or just when you remember it? Make prayer a part of your daily routine. God wants to hear from you. One other thing I ask from God is for patience. I am a very impatient person. I want things right away. When something comes to my mind, I want to fulfill it immediately. Hebrews 10:36 says, "Patient endurance is what you need now, so that you will continue to do God's will. Then you will receive all that he has promised." God's peaceful reminder is to simply ask God when we need something. He is always listening.

DAY 76
Live in Peace

Do all that you can to live in peace with everyone.
—Romans 12:18 (NLT)

We all have the best intentions to live in peace with everyone, but then someone makes us mad or hurts our feelings. If our feelings are hurt, it may take a while for us to forgive the other person. If we are mad, we also need to forgive the other person. God wants us to forgive one another so that he can forgive us of our sins. God's peaceful reminder is that we should live in peace with everyone. Just think how much better this world would be with everyone living in peace.

Philippians 4:7 says, "Then you will experience God's peace, which exceeds anything we can understand. His peace will guard your hearts and minds as you live in Christ Jesus." Whenever we are struggling, we need to turn to God, and he will give us peace in our hearts and minds. God is so good. Living in this world, it is good to know that we have this peace from God. "Do all that you can to live in peace with everyone."

DAY 77
Friendship

Wise words bring many benefits, and hard work brings rewards.
—Proverbs 12:14 (NLT)

I asked myself, *What is something that takes a lot of hard work?* The first thing that came to mind is friendship. Friendships require hard work. We need to invest in our relationships with our friends. If we don't, these relationships will fall apart. We must be disciplined and schedule time with one another on a regular basis. I love scheduling monthly get-togethers with my friends. We usually go out to dinner or sometimes breakfast. I love catching up with my friends. My friends always have wise words for me. The verse above says, "Wise words bring many benefits." I am so lucky to have many great friends in my life. I love their companionship and wise words.

Galatians 6:2 says, "Share each other's burdens, and in this way obey the law of Christ." Friends know how to share our burdens. Sharing our burdens allows our friends to try to help us through the tough times we are experiencing. Thessalonians 5:11 says, "So encourage each other and build each other up, just as you are already doing." As friends, we should encourage and build one another up. We should provide supportive words and help one another out. We are meant to have great friendships. Do you have great friends?

But you, dear friends, must build each other up in your most holy faith, pray in the power of the Holy Spirit, and await the mercy of our Lord Jesus Christ, who will bring you eternal life.

—Jude 20–21 (NLT)

One of my goals for the new year is to start a Bible Study group at our church. I have been studying the Bible alone since 2014. I think I would learn more by doing a group study. I have also followed many people on Instagram who are doing Bible studies. I am learning so much from them. Together we will "build each other up in your most holy faith." Remember when I talked about buying a lot of stuff on Amazon and that books and highlighters were my weaknesses. The many books that I buy are Bible related. I own many Bibles. I also own many Bible reference books.

I recently found a company called The Daily Grace Co. They have many Bible studies that you can buy. I have already gone through Colossians, and tonight, I just finished James. These Bible studies have been a game changer. Each day, the study allows me to focus on a few verses of the book. Then there is a short reading and some questions to answer. How do you build others up with your faith?

DAY 79
Skill

*I know all the things you do. I have seen your love, your
faith, your service, and your patient endurance.*
—Revelation 2:19 (NLT)

I started playing the clarinet in fourth grade. I wanted to play the
flute, but it just didn't work out. I practiced pretty much every day.
I also went to band camp in the summer, where I learned a lot. I ended
up playing the clarinet until my freshman year of college, and then I
never played it again. I am forty-four years old, and I am thinking about
buying a new clarinet so that I can pick it back up again. Will my skill
come back easily, or will I have to relearn everything again?

When I was a child, I used to ice-skate much of the time. In the
winter, our gravel driveway was covered in ice, and I skated up and
down it. I loved it. A few weeks ago, we went ice-skating at an arena.
I was so excited to get my skates back on (I had kept my ice skates all
those years). When I got on the ice, I realized that I had lost my skill. I
barely made it around the ring. I was sad. Have you lost a skill? Do you
want to pick it up again? What are you waiting for?

DAY 80
Photography

When I see the rainbow in the clouds, I will remember the eternal covenant between God and every living creature on earth.
—Genesis 9:16 (NLT)

I love photography. I love taking photos of nature, especially rainbows, sunrises, and sunsets. God creates these beautiful scenes for us to enjoy. We should take time to notice these stunning views and not take them for granted. When you are having a bad day, walk outside to enjoy God's beauty. Stop to smell the flowers or admire a butterfly. These are God's peaceful reminders. Take time to breathe in the fresh air and enjoy the sunshine on your face.

As I write this, it is winter and currently nineteen degrees outside. When the sun shines on the snow, it just sparkles. It is so pretty. After a big storm, I love seeing a rainbow in the sky. I am a very anxious person. When thunderstorms occur, I am a nervous wreck. When they occur at night, I can't sleep. When severe weather comes my way, I can't relax until the storm has passed. However, when the storm passes and reveals a rainbow, this is God's peaceful reminder that he is always watching over us, especially during the storms of life. We can always count on God. What part of nature do you like to notice and admire?

DAY 81
College Days

The Lord is my strength and my song; he has given me victory. This is my God, and I will praise him—my father's God, and I will exalt him!
—Exodus 15:2 (NLT)

When I went to college, I was nervous to be away from my family and boyfriend. During this time, I stopped going to church completely. I am still upset at myself for doing this. I prayed every night before bed but felt like I didn't have to attend church. While at college, I studied a lot. My major was animal science, and my plan was to become a large-animal veterinarian. I studied many hours every night. On the weekends, I went home to see my boyfriend (who is now my husband). I ended up getting all As during my first semester of college. What a victory that was! I remember praying to God to help me get good grades. "The Lord is my strength."

Psalm 28:7 says, "The Lord is my strength and shield. I trust him with all my heart. He helps me, and my heart is filled with joy. I burst out in songs of thanksgiving." One Sunday during my college days, I decided to go to the Catholic church on campus. I remember singing the songs and being moved to tears. As I think back on this memory, I realize how happy God must have been to see me again in his church. I was away for a long time, and then I came back. To be honest, I wasn't a regular churchgoer until well into my adult years. When I think back on the decisions I made, I am sad that church wasn't the center of my world. God should always be the center of our worlds. During your lifetime, did you ever fall away from the church? Take time to reflect on it.

DAY 82
Twenty Minutes

May the Lord bless you and protect you. May the Lord smile on you and be gracious to you. May the Lord show you his favor and give you his peace.

—NUMBERS 6:24–26 (NLT)

I already told you that I was born three months prematurely, but I didn't tell you the whole story. When I was born, the doctor told my parents that I would only live for twenty minutes. My whole life was only supposed to be twenty minutes long. I am now forty-four years old. I was in the NICU for two and a half months. I was also baptized twice, once in the hospital and once in church.

The verse above says, "May the Lord bless you and protect you. May the Lord smile on you and be gracious to you." I am here because of God. He saved me for a reason. I am so blessed. My parents called me the miracle baby. Psalm 106:4 says, "Remember me, Lord, when you show favor to your people; come near and rescue me." The Lord rescued me when I was a baby and when I had my midlife crisis. God is so good. Do you have a life-changing story? Share it with someone today.

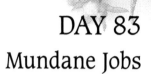

DAY 83
Mundane Jobs

Serve only the Lord your God and fear him alone. Obey
his commands, listen to his voice, and cling to him.
—Deuteronomy 13:4 (NLT)

I dislike doing the dishes and grocery shopping. I dislike both with a passion. I wish my husband would do these jobs so that I wouldn't have to. However, we discussed this. He said, "Sure, I will do those jobs, but then you have to mow the lawn and shovel snow." Um, no thank you. Guess I am stuck doing the dishes and grocery shopping. Even though I dislike these jobs, I should feel honored to do them. They help me take care of my family, which is a gift from God.

Philippians 2:14 says, "Do everything without complaining and arguing." When I was a child, I lived on my family's dairy farm. The two jobs I complained the most about were picking up stones in the fields and baling hay in the summer. I disliked these jobs because they took forever to do. We spent hours in the fields picking up stones. We also spent hours unloading bales of hay from the wagons in summer. Again, I should feel honored to do these jobs, as we were taking care of our dairy cows. Are there certain chores or jobs you do not like to do?

DAY 84
Farm Chores

*This is my command—be strong and courageous! Do not be afraid
or discouraged. For the Lord your God is with you wherever you go.*
—Joshua 1:9 (NLT)

I grew up on my family's dairy farm. We had to do farm chores daily.
I started out doing simple chores like feeding the cows or spreading
lime in the main aisle. Working on the farm made me strong. During
my teen years, I helped my dad milk cows every night. I was glad that
I grew up on a dairy farm. It taught me how to work hard, and I was
happy to spend time with my family.

First Corinthians 3:8 says, "The one who plants and the one who
waters work together with the same purpose. And both will be rewarded
for their own hard work." Another peaceful reminder from God is
Romans 12:11, which says, "Never be lazy, but work hard and serve
the Lord enthusiastically." We are doing everything for the Lord. We
should happily do our chores because we are doing them for the Lord.
What was your childhood like? What is your favorite memory from
childhood?

DAY 85
Homebody

For this world is not our permanent home; we are looking forward to a home yet to come.

—Hebrews 13:14 (NLT)

I am a homebody. I love to stay home and in sweatpants and a sweatshirt—oh, and slippers. If I could plan my perfect day, it would be a day at my house. I would sleep in until 7:00 a.m. and then drink a pot of tea while watching *Good Day Wisconsin* on television. Next, I would do my Bible readings and devotionals. Then I would bake some cookies—oatmeal of course. Later I would play a board or card game with my family. I might take a nap on the couch or watch a movie on television. If nothing good was on TV, we would put in *Little House on the Prairie*, as we have the whole series on DVD. I would go to bed at 9:30 p.m. It would be a great day. If you could plan your perfect day, what would it look like? Who would you spend your time with?

DAY 86
Defeated

I will bless the Lord who guides me; even at night my
heart instructs me. I know the Lord is always with me.
I will not be shaken, for he is right beside me.
—Psalm 16:7–8 (NLT)

L ast night, I had a dream that I was working in a bakery and frosting a huge sheet cake for a customer. In my dream, I kept messing up, and the cake looked horrible. I was devastated that I couldn't make it look eye pleasing. I woke up and felt defeated like I had failed. That sick feeling you get in the pit of your stomach stuck with me the entire day. This dream made me realize just how afraid I was of failing. I have perfectionist tendencies. If it's not perfect, I want to throw it away. However, making mistakes is how we learn the best. Ask God for help. "I will bless the Lord who guides me …I know the Lord is always with me." Do you remember your dreams? Do you forget about them right away? Do your dreams tell you something about yourself?

DAY 87
Don't Sweat the Small Stuff

The heartfelt counsel of a friend is as sweet as perfume and incense.
—Proverbs 27:9 (NLT)

My previous boss, Rene, is also my friend. She is wise, and she has taught me so much about life. She would always say, "Don't sweat the small stuff." My perfectionist tendencies got the better of me sometimes. Whenever I got overwhelmed with my work tasks, I could always go to her, and she would help me prioritize what needed to get done and what could wait. In my young working years, I made everything a priority, which made work stressful for me. Rene helped me see that not everything could be a priority. She would also encourage a good work-life balance.

When I was young, I was a workaholic. I loved working and lost track of time every afternoon. I got home late, which then delayed suppertime. It was a stressful cycle, but she taught me to have a good work-life balance. "Leave work at work." Thank you, Rene, for teaching me throughout the years. Do you have a great friend who counsels you? Give that friend a call today.

DAY 88
Peaceful Week

So I recommend having fun, because there is nothing better
for people in this world than to eat, drink, and enjoy life.
That way they will experience some happiness along with
all the hard work God gives them under the sun.

—ECCLESIASTES 8:15 (NLT)

E very New Year's Eve, my family likes to stay home and play darts in our living room. I always make a charcuterie board for supper with meat, cheese, nuts, and fruit. We look forward to it every year. I always take off work between Christmas and New Year's. During that week, I like to "eat, drink, and enjoy life." The kids and I also like to play games and just relax. It's such a peaceful week to enjoy my family.

When I was a child, my family and all my relatives on my mom's side got together at Plamann Park for Memorial Day. We grilled out, played Frisbee golf, and went to the petting zoo. Sometimes the whole family played kickball. It was fun in the sun. Do you have any family traditions? Reflect on them now.

DAY 89
Bunion Surgery

He does great things too marvelous to understand.
He performs countless miracles.
—Job 5:9 (NLT)

I had bunion surgery on my right foot in 2013. I used a kneeling scooter to get around, as I could not put any weight on my foot for a few weeks. Using one leg to only to get around was a tough adjustment. Before this surgery, I took it for granted that I could walk on both feet. Have you ever had an experience where you lost the ability to use an arm or a leg? How did you feel? Did it challenge you each day to complete simple tasks?

It is so easy for us to take everything we have for granted until we suddenly lose it. In the book of Job, Job faced many difficult trials, but he never stopped trusting God. We should also trust God in all our sufferings and trials. We need to thank God daily for our ability to walk, talk, eat, see, and hear. These are gifts from God.

DAY 90
Nighttime Reading

Jesus replied, "But even more blessed are all who hear the word of God and put it into practice."
—LUKE 11:28 (NLT)

Every night before bed, I read Bible devotionals to my kids. Currently, we are reading *Our Daily Bread for Kids: 365 Meaningful Moments with God* by Crystal Bowman and Teri McKinley. We are also reading *The Bible Made Easy for Kids* by Dave Strehler. Do we read every night? No, but we try to read at least five times a week. I started these Bible readings with my kids when they were four and two years old. I read to them while they took their bath. My kids learned how to make the sign of the cross while taking a bath. I love these precious moments before bed. God's peaceful reminders are read and heard.

We all need some peace before going to sleep. As the verse above says, "But even more blessed are all who hear the word of God and put it into practice." If you have children, do you read to them before bed? If you don't have children, do you read before bed? What peaceful practice do you do before bed?

DAY 91
2023 Goals

Never be lazy, but work hard and serve the Lord enthusiastically.
—ROMANS 12:11 (NLT)

I have many personal goals for 2023. My daily goals are to read my devotionals and daily Bible readings of the Catholic church, to listen to the *Catechism of the Catholic Church* podcast, and do Pilates. My weekly goals are preparing for mass, family game nights, and editing my book. My monthly goals are to go on a date night with my husband, spend time with friends, and clean the house. My main goal for 2023 is to publish this book. I am one week in, and I am exhausted. I think I have overcommitted myself for 2023.

The Bible says to "work hard and serve the Lord enthusiastically." It is now March 2023, and here's an update on my 2023 goals: I stopped listening to the *Catechism of the Catholic Church* podcast and doing Pilates. It's OK to reflect on your goals and get rid of the ones that don't feel right in this season. I wish I could be superhuman, but I am not. I think my goals feel good now. I don't feel overwhelmed like I did in January. Do you have any goals for 2023? How are they going? Do you think you can maintain your goals throughout the year? Why or why not?

DAY 92
A Cheerful Giver

You must each decide in your heart how much to give.
And don't give reluctantly or in response to pressure.
For God loves a person who gives cheerfully.
—2 Corinthians 9:7 (NLT)

I haven't folded a towel in years because our kids always fold all the towels in our house. Our kids have daily chores that they must complete. The kids also help with drying the dishes after dinner. My son mows the grass during the summer months. He just started his first job. He works as a busboy and dishwasher at a supper club in our hometown.

We all must learn to be cheerful givers of our time and talents. We must be willing to share our gifts and to help others. The Bible tells us to help others and to use our time and talents for the benefit of others. Matthew 5:16 says, "In the same way, let your good deeds shine out for all to see, so that everyone will praise your heavenly Father." When I think about good deeds, I think about the corporal works of mercy. Feed the hungry, give drink to the thirsty, clothe the naked, give shelter to the homeless, visit the sick and imprisoned, and bury the dead. Do you use your time and talents to help others, or do you hide your talents? God created us with talents so that we could help others. Use them wisely.

DAY 93
Ask God

Don't act thoughtlessly, but understand what the Lord wants you to do.
—EPHESIANS 5:17 (NLT)

I have always wanted to have my own baking show on television. Ever since I was young, I have loved watching cooking shows. Whenever I have spare time, I am found in the kitchen baking something delicious for my family. I love making different kinds of cookies and muffins. Baking is my way to relax. It's my outlet.

However, after talking with God, I see that he wants me to write this book. I don't think the baking show is in his plans for me, and that's OK. Do you ever consult God about what to do next? If you don't consult him, why not? Would you rather be in control? Jeremiah 42:3 says, "Pray that the Lord your God will show us what to do and where to go." We should always follow God's plan and not our own. The next time you don't know what to do, consult with God. He is waiting for you. He wants to guide and help you.

DAY 94
Isolated

Don't love money; be satisfied with what you have. For God has said, "I will never fail you, I will never abandon you."
—Hebrews 13:5 (NLT)

I will never forget the day when COVID-19 hit our country. I was watching TV. When I heard the president of the United States say that we were in a pandemic, I cried so hard. I was scared. Life as we knew it was over. Everyone started working from home. The kids started virtual school. We watched church online. If we did go out, we had to wear masks. It was devastating to me that we could not see people's smiles. During this time, I knew that God would never abandon us. My family became very isolated. I missed seeing family, friends, and coworkers. I missed going to the grocery store (I only did online pickup orders). When the COVID-19 vaccines came out, I immediately got in line to get mine. The vaccines were a breath of fresh air. Slowly but surely, we started seeing family and friends again.

What emotions did you go through when the pandemic hit? Did you miss your family, friends, and coworkers? Did you miss going to church or the grocery store? Hebrews states, "Don't love money; be satisfied with what you have." This is God's peaceful reminder that we should be happy with what we have. We should not constantly want new things just because the world is creating them. Another good reminder is not comparing your life to someone else's. Comparison can leave us feeling unhappy and down. Be happy with what you have because everything you have is a gift from God. He knows what you need and when you need it. God is good.

DAY 95
Bipolar Disorder

For the Lamb on the throne will be their Shepherd.
He will lead them to springs of life-giving water. And
God will wipe every tear from their eyes.

—Revelation 7:17 (NLT)

I was diagnosed with bipolar disorder in 2020. I would have extreme ups and downs. When I was up, I had a hard time sleeping, as I had so much energy that I didn't know what to do with myself. I wanted to do everything and never stop to take a breath. I stayed up until midnight for many nights of the week and only slept for a few hours every night. However, when I was down, it was scary. I was very depressed, and it was hard to do anything. I didn't want to do anything but sleep. I had a hard time doing normal tasks like working, washing the dishes, and making dinner. I didn't even want to take a shower. It was awful. In 2020, I went on medication, and I became a whole new person. I no longer have ups and downs. I feel like I am on a normal wavelength and steady wavelength.

The verse above says, "And God will wipe every tear from their eyes." God was there for me when I needed help. He wiped the tears from my eyes. Isaiah 41:10 says, "Don't be afraid, for I am with you. Don't be discouraged, for I am your God. I will strengthen you and help you. I will hold you up with my victorious right hand." God is our strength. He can get us through our tough situations. Have you ever gone through a debilitating medical condition? How did you get through it?

DAY 96
Reading Goal

God is my strong fortress, and he makes my way perfect.
—2 Samuel 22:33 (NLT)

The last few years, I have set a reading goal. Last year, my goal was to read twelve books. I ended up reading nineteen books. Since I am writing this book, I decided not to set a reading goal for 2023. I follow many booklovers on social media, and many people read over one hundred books a year. I find this number to be very impressive. Sometimes social media makes me feel like I am not doing enough with my days, especially when I see other people's goals. However, I need to remember that God makes my way perfect. I am doing enough. I am living out my days well and the way God wants me to. Ultimately, God's plan wins. Do you like to read? Do you have a reading goal each year that you try to attain?

DAY 97
A Hard Time

Give your burdens to the Lord, and he will take care of
you. He will not permit the godly to slip and fall.
—Psalm 55:22 (NLT)

In 2014, I struggled with life. I had a hard time putting one foot in front of the other. All I wanted to do was sleep. I debated about what my purpose in life was. I felt like I had no purpose. It was an awful feeling. After getting some help, I decided to start reading the Bible. The Bible is the best self-help book you can read. I opened my Bible up every night and started reading it. I read it slowly and consistently. It took me nineteen months to read the whole Bible from cover to cover. In that time, God healed my heart and spoke to me. He told me that he was preparing me for something special. I wondered why God chose me—someone so broken in this season of life. He told me to keep reading. So I did just that.

Did you ever go through an extremely difficult time in your life? How did you get out of it, or are you still struggling with it? Ask God to help you. "Give your burdens to the Lord, and he will take care of you." What burdens can you give to the Lord today?

DAY 98
The Greatest Commandments

Jesus replied, "You must love the Lord your God with all your heart, all your soul, and all your mind." This is the first and greatest commandment. A second is equally important: "Love your neighbor as yourself."

—Matthew 22:37–39 (NLT)

These are the greatest of all the commandments. We should love the Lord first, even above our families. God should be number one in our lives. He made us and the whole world. For that, we should be very grateful each day. Do you love God first? We should also love our neighbor as ourselves. This means we need to love ourselves before we can spread love to others around us. Do you love yourself, or do you cut yourself down? We should be kind to ourselves. Rest when you need rest. Work hard at your place of employment. Think positive thoughts throughout the day. Take care of your body by exercising and eating healthy.

God paid a good price for us, and we should take care of our body in return. Once we love ourselves, then we should love our neighbors. We love our neighbors by bringing them cookies or mowing their grass. We smile at strangers when at the grocery store. We help those in need—the sick and the poor. What is one way you can love your neighbor today?

DAY 99
Guard Your Heart

Guard your heart above all else, for it determines the course of your life.
—PROVERBS 4:23 (NLT)

When I was in high school, my heart was broken by a boy. I thought my life was ruined. I was sad and then angry. I cried many tears. Then I was mad that this boy was interested in other girls. God knew this boy was not meant to be my husband. He could see it before I could.

The quote, "Everything happens for a reason," crosses my mind. I firmly believe that everything happens for a reason. The hard part is that we usually don't understand why something is happening to us until much later. God knows what is good for us and what is not. Proverbs 15:13 says, "A glad heart makes a happy face; a broken heart crushes the spirit." Even though my spirit was crushed for weeks, I eventually recovered and became happy again. It is human nature to want to protect our hearts. We don't like getting our hearts broken. A broken heart is an awful feeling to have. God can fix our broken hearts. God will always love us. Did you ever go through a heartbreak? How did you get through it?

DAY 100
Chicago

When doubts filled my mind, your comfort
gave me renewed hope and cheer.
—Psalm 94:19 (NLT)

Many years back, my mom and I traveled to Chicago to see my brother. I was afraid to go to a big city. I grew up on a dairy farm in the country outside of a very small town. Big cities scared me. There were so many people and cars that it was all overwhelming. I was scared to walk around because I thought someone would attack us. While we were there, we enjoyed some deep-dish pizza. We couldn't eat the whole pizza. There were some homeless people across the street, so my brother gave our leftover pizza to one gentleman. He was extremely grateful. Our trip turned out well, and we were safe.

The verse above says, "When doubts filled my mind, your comfort gave me renewed hope and cheer." Have you ever traveled to a place you were unsure of? How did you feel? How did you overcome your fear? I hope this book has given you comfort and cheer over the past one hundred days. I hope you became closer to God during this time and got to know more about yourself too. God has many peaceful reminders. We just need to watch for them. Remember, God loves you and always will.

NOTE

Day 10 and 26

1. "Kindness." Yahoo. Accessed on July 25, 2023. <u>kindness definition yahoo - Search (bing.com)</u>

Printed in the United States
by Baker & Taylor Publisher Services